introduction to
fashion
illustrating

introduction to
fashion
illustrating

WRITTEN AND ILLUSTRATED
BY ANN STEPHENSON

FAIRCHILD PUBLICATIONS
NEW YORK

Edited by Olga Kontzias

Layout executed by Millie Rodriguez

Standard Book Number: 87005-369-8

Library of Congress Catalog Card Number: 80-70881

Printed in the United States of America

…in memory of my sister Betty Jean Williams

An Opening Chat

For some time now, I have been aware of the need for a current and more comprehensive book on fashion illustration. A book that would be more helpful and practical in guiding young artists seeking a career in department store advertising.

Fashion illustration is a large and exciting field, and offers a high degree of creativity. Fashion art is used in practically every phase of department store advertising — in newspapers, magazines, catalogs, direct mail, billboards, posters and yes, even television. It is a business where the art is designed purposely and drawn in such a way as to create *sales*.

There are many career opportunities for fashion illustrators, as it is the largest commercial art field an artist can enter. Every day fashion artwork is seen in newspapers across the country. In small cities and large metropolitan areas hundreds of stores employ artists who create a consistent fashion image for that store and a definite style for themselves. Millions of dollars are spent every year by department stores alone on newspaper advertising.

In addition to department stores, the fashion artist can seek opportunities as a staff or freelance artist, with specialty shops, fashion syndicates, fashion manufacturers; and with advertising agencies and studios who handle fashion accounts.

Introduction to Fashion Illustrating is concerned primarily with setting forth the foundations and fundamentals of drawing fashion art for women, men and children. It will deal with information relating to fashion proportions, how to merchandise clothing, and how to render fabrics and textures.

Before any results can be achieved with fashion illustration, control of the artist's materials must be acquired and techniques for obtaining desired effects must be learned. I have devoted the introductory unit to the types of artist's materials needed for fashion illustration and to the step-by-step techniques for wash drawings and line and wash drawings.

Any student with comparatively good artistic ability *and the desire* can be a fashion artist. It is presupposed that such a student will have already studied and will continue to research the many fine books available on anatomy. For of course, anatomy is the basic for all fashion illustration.

I do not profess to know more than any other fashion artist, nor do I contend that "my way" is better. The intention of this book from start to finish is to lend you a hand towards your future. This is a profession at which I have spent many years. And I have loved it from my toes up!

I wish to thank Roger A. Stephenson who took the photographs of the artist's materials in Unit 1. The fashion photographs were generously contributed by Gregg Hagley, Advertising Manager at Rogers Department Store, Grand Rapids, Michigan. I thank Kathy VanKalker who posed for the fashion photographs and Rogers Department Store for the merchandise used in these photographs. National Correct Color, Grand Rapids, Michigan, kindly supplied the halftone dot patterns for the last unit.

My warmest thanks to Georgia Waite for her help in preparing the manuscript. And to Marie Meyer and Gregg Hagley for their encouragement when I needed it the most.

Lowell, Michigan   Ann Stephenson
April 1981

Contents

1 Introduction to Fashion Illustrating

Creating Fashion Illustrations

Whether it is making a wash drawing or a simple line drawing, learning to control the artist's materials and tools is a very important skill for any artist wanting to create fashion illustrations.

This control allows you to develop your own style and technique. And knowing how to use these materials will help you get the best possible reproduction in newspaper advertising.

Current fashion magazines play an important part in a fashion illustrator's work. There you will find all the information you need on any garment you wish to illustrate. You will be able to keep up with the latest fashion, hair styles and accessories. Develop a classified file of fashion photographs of both black and white models. For you will use both in your work. And from major newspapers, clip other fashion illustrators' work to see how they handle their technique. This is an important part of learning to draw fashions.

The fashion reference file plays a major role in any fashion artist's busy day, for there is the source of your strength. You will be only as good as your files.

Department stores have to gear their advertising to meet newspaper deadlines, and almost everything is done at high speed, under pressure and being rushed at certain seasons. This is where your reference file comes in. At your fingertips are many great poses to pick from in a hurry.

Speed becomes a great asset to the artist in retail store advertising, and the ability to work under pressure and still turn out quality work makes you a very valuable person.

How to Start Your Reference File

Starting your reference file can be quite simple. It may take a while to develop a large one, but begin by buying monthly issues of leading fashion magazines.

Refer to fashion poses in Unit 2 for help in deciding if a photograph is usable. Clip photographs of heads, hands and feet, as well as photographs of the whole body.

Even as the photographs get old, and the styles become outdated, the body remains the same. It is a simple matter to change a hair-do and lower or raise a hemline.

Save photographs that suggest an idea that you might use with another photograph. For example, scuba diving goggles to use with an ad on swimwear.

Keep the filing system simple. *Do not* make too many categories. You will, after a few years, develop a memory file, and will know just where and what you have on file.

The chart illustrated here is a guide to help you start a filing system that is easy to work with and simple.

Use 9" x 11½" standard file folders. Use a folder for each entry listed on the chart.

Trim excess paper away from the photographs and always fold the photograph you are saving to face outward. This is a time-saving system, for it eliminates picking up and unfolding every photograph on file to find what you need.

WOMEN	accessories: hats, gloves, handbags, jewelry, cosmetics, shoes bridal, formals, gowns, robes, dresses coats, sportswear, suits, pantsuits, furs swimwear, bras, girdles, blouses, sweaters, slacks
MEN	suits, slacks, hats, shirts, sweaters, underwear, pajamas, robes, ties, jewelry, socks, slippers, shoes, gloves, coats, sport coats
CHILDREN	girls: playclothes, dresses, outerwear, sportswear, nightclothes, underwear, gloves boys: playclothes, shirts, sweaters, underwear, nightclothes, slacks, outerwear
MISCELLANEOUS	sports equipment, scenery, furniture, floral decorations, Christmas decorations and other holiday items

The Fashion Artist's Materials

The basic drawing materials used by fashion artists are the same as any commercial artist. There are many brands to select from, and any beginning artist should seek help from a local art dealer in their selection.

Pencils Select a mechanical lead holder and at least three grades of lead to work with. Use a soft lead, #2B, for your preliminary pencil sketches, and a hard lead, #2H, to transfer your final pencil drawing onto your work area. I recommend a lead holder over buying pencils for its economy, as well as the ease involved in keeping a sharp point of the lead through the use of a sand pad.

Tracing Paper Pad A thin transparent tracing paper for practice work, as well as being used to work out the fashion figure before transferring it onto the work area. It is easy to slip your first drawing under the next sheet and work out the final drawing that you intend to use.

Ink Always use black India waterproof ink for wash drawings and line work. It is transparent and reproduces well. It will not run when you paint a wash over ink line work, or over another wash area.

Brushes Select quality pointed sable water-color brushes. Good brushes are important to the artist who wants to master the wash technique and render fashion textures. Brush point numbers 0, 2, 4 and 5 are most often used for fashion art.

Palette There are plastic and porcelain palettes available with round and rectangular wells to use in holding ink and water to mix for your wash drawings.

Pen Points For your ink line work you can use a crowquill pen holder and several pen points in medium and fine points. Also available for line work is the popular rapidograph pen. It comes in a cartridge pen holder and has many point sizes to choose from.

Illustration Boards A paper that has a heavy cardboard base is required for wash drawings. The thickness of the illustration board will absorb an ink wash, where a thin sheet of paper will buckle and the surface will become uneven when a wash is applied. The board is available in several surfaces—smooth, medium and coarse. Numbers 100 and 300 are most popular.

Kneaded Eraser A soft eraser that will clean up your pencil work without leaving dirty smudges. After your illustration has been completed, using gentle strokes, you can clean up any pencil marks you might have overlooked.

Other Supplies Other supplies you will need in your work as a fashion artist are *masking tape,* used to block off work areas for wash drawings; *glasses* or *cups* to hold clean water to use for wash drawings; a *paint cloth* to clean your brushes; a *roll of gray transfer paper* to trace your pencil drawing onto the illustration board; *sand pads* to keep the pencil lead sharpened to a point; *white retouch paint,* an opaque mixture to use for texture work.

Rendering Fashion Art in Ink with Pen & Brush

Learning to use ink with pen and brush for fashion illustrations can be very satisfying for the artist.

This technique, referred to as line, is made up of solid black lines or areas. The lines are achieved by using a crowquill pen, a rapidograph pen or brushes and India ink. The medium is popular because you can create the effect of textures in fashion with a variety of lines. Lines that can show the softness of fur to the rough texture of tweed. It is an important skill to develop because fashion line drawings are always in demand. And it reproduces well for newspapers as well as magazines.

Painting Fashion Art in Wash

Learning to use wash in fashion illustration is as exciting as it is rewarding. This is the favorite medium for many fashion artists.

Wash is the mixing of India ink with water. The various shades of gray are determined by the amount of water used in diluting the ink.

The wash technique is a spontaneous medium. Once the wash technique has been mastered it is easy to work with. And can be used to create the textures in fashion in many different ways.

Wash dries quickly and evenly, allowing the artist to work fast in small areas as well as in large background areas.

The medium reproduces well for newspapers when it is used with a value range of three shades of gray, black and white. See tonal chart on page 121. For magazine illustrations it is excellent, having a full range of tone much like a photograph.

It takes a lot of patience in learning to put down a good wash drawing. Do not rush, practice and experiment.

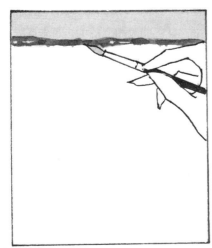

1 Keep the brush full of wash to form a puddle as you slowly work across the paper several times—left to right—right to left—slowly moving down the area.

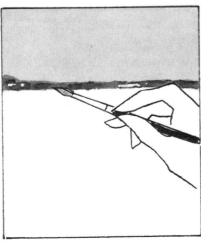

2 *Do not* allow the brush to run dry. Keep it wet and the puddle even.

Mastering a Flat Wash

Many fashion techniques require that you paint a smooth, single shade of gray flat tone. Once the work area has been marked off, begin by starting at the top lefthand corner and moving steadily, but not too fast, across the work area (as indicated in artwork). This is a very exasperating medium and it is easy to become discouraged—but with practice you will soon be pleased with the results.

Prepare a small bowl of water with ink for a light shade of gray.

3 Using the left to right—right to left motion "pulling" the puddle. Never work over an area that has already been finished.

4 Keep a paint cloth handy (a clean baby diaper is great) as you will need to dry the brush.

5 Soak up the puddle of wash as you reach the bottom of the work area with the dry brush.

Painting the Fashion Figure in Ink & Wash

Always work out the fashion drawing on tracing paper carefully before transferring it on the work area. This is important because to get a clean flat wash one must keep the board free of excessive pencil smudges and finger marks.

Ink in the figure first, using a brush, crowquill pen or both. When it is finished, the line drawing is now ready to lay a flat wash.

Using one shade of gray wash, begin at the neckline and slowly work back and forth—keeping the brush wet and always allowing the puddle to "pull along." *Do not rush.* As long as there is a puddle of wash one can work at a comfortable speed.

When the wash is at the hemline, wipe the brush dry with the paint cloth and then clean up the remaining puddle.

A Step-by-Step Wash Drawing

In this bridal illustration, the figure was carefully transferred onto the illustration board. A flat wash, the lightest tone to be used, is applied to the flesh tone, veil and some folds of the gown. The white paper will be used for much of the gown.

To get the effect of softness in the folds and flow of the gown and veil, the second darkest tone is now applied. This tone is also used for shadow areas under the chin line, armholes and hair-do.

13

Using drafting tape, the next step is to mask off the background with tape and apply the flat wash, working slowly and keeping "a puddle" for a smooth finish. Once the background is completely dried, remove the tape and you will have a clean edge around your artwork.

The third and darkest tone will be used for the accent areas around the bows, underarm and hair-do. This is also the tone used for the lace detail on the gown, carefully applied with a fine brush and crowquill pen point.

Painting the Fashion Head in Wash

When rendering the fashion head in wash remember that for newspaper reproduction you can use three shades of gray, white and black. See tonal chart on page 121.

Begin always with the lightest shade first, laying the flat wash over the entire area.

When it is completely dry, add the second shade of gray, using this to shade the shadow areas around the eyes, cheeks and nose.

The third shade of gray should be used carefully. To maintain the softness of features it is used to shape the lips, eyeballs, nostrils and to highlight the hair.

For the final highlight, use black ink. As you see here—it is used carefully around the eyes, lips and hair.

2 Illustrating Women's Fashions

Drawing the Female Fashion Figure

The artist who wants to be a successful fashion illustrator should be able to draw the human figure and draw it well. Drawing clothing will be much more convincing if you know the form beneath them. In department store advertising the fashion artist is, in a sense, a silent salesperson. In newspaper ads the artwork must give the fashion information at a glance. The illustration must stop the reader and make her want to look and feel like the woman in the illustration. Surveys indicate that you have only three seconds to stop the eye before it goes on to the next page. In merchandising fashion you should try to pinpoint your potential customer. Always consider *who* is going to wear this garment, *what* is she like, and *why* is she going to wear it.

The next pages deal with information relating to fashion proportions, how to merchandise clothing, and how to render fabrics and textures.

These important facts about fashion illustration are basic and invaluable. Study the information and learn to control the mediums, for the rewards are well worth the effort.

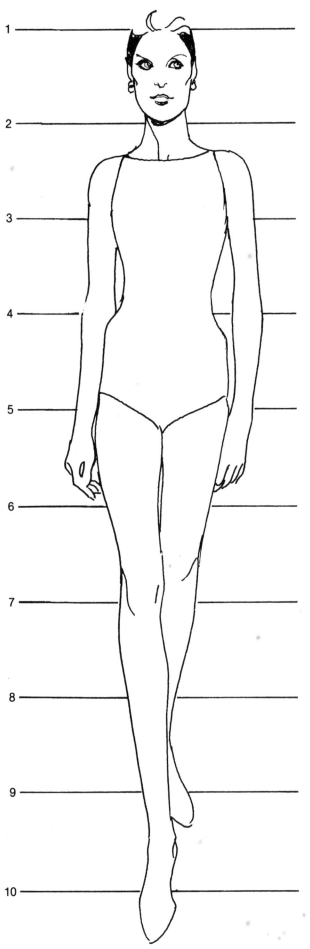

Proportions of the Ideal Female Fashion Figure

The figures at the right show the proportions of the ideal fashion figure. To express the elegance and glamour of fashion art the figure is 8½ heads tall. Drawing the fashion figure as much as 9 to 9½, and even 10 heads high is acceptable.

The ideal fashion figure is sometimes a tricky thing to achieve. A lot of customers are selective about their choice of an "ideal" model, for every woman shopping for clothes wants to be beautiful and attractive. They seem to prefer models they can emulate and look up to. If the woman is overweight she will reject any model who reminds her of her own characteristics. This is an important rule to remember when drawing the half size and queen size figures.

NORMAL   FASHION

20

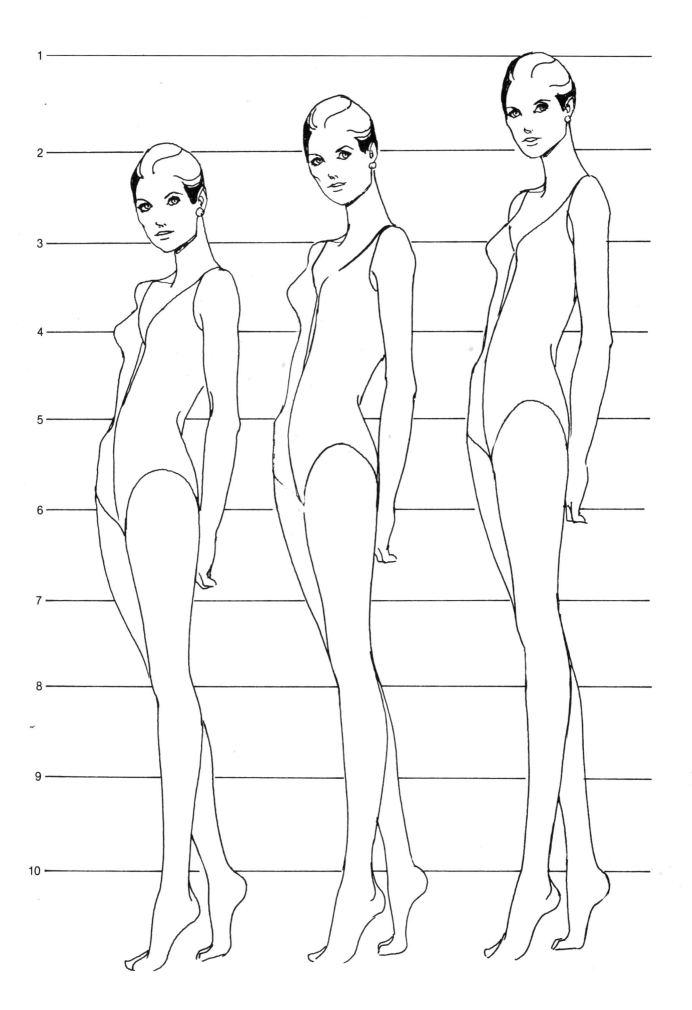

1

2

3

4

5

6

7

8

9

10

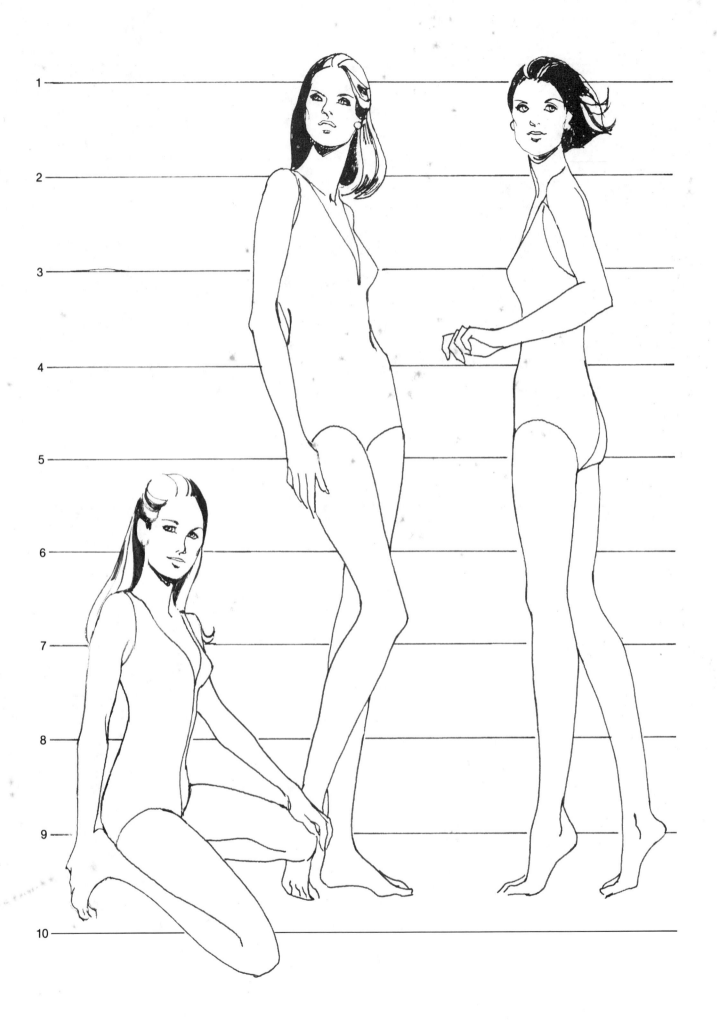

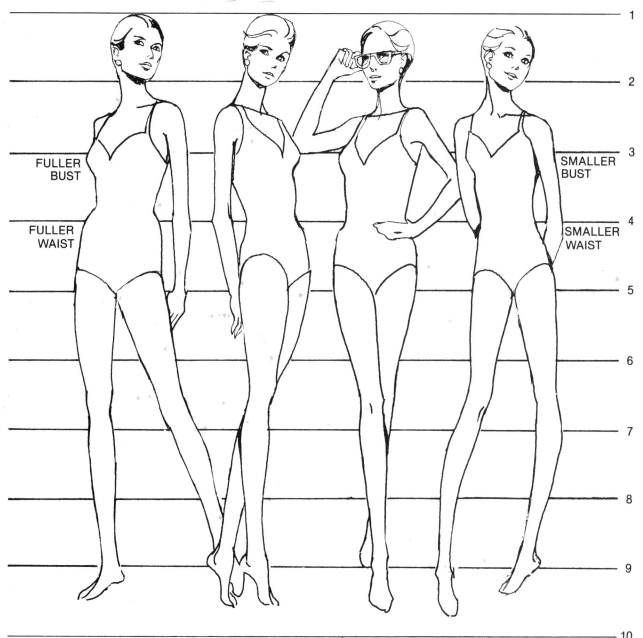

FULLER BUST

FULLER WAIST

SMALLER BUST

SMALLER WAIST

1

2

3

4

5

6

7

8

9

10

HALF SIZE & QUEEN SIZE FIGURE   FASHIONABLE FIGURE   JUNIOR FIGURE

Proportions for Various Size Groups

For the artist, the height of the head is the unit of measurement for the entire body. Using this method the chart above will show you the ideal fashion proportions for different size groups. The height of the fashion figure is 8½ heads high. Keep the head on a long slender neck. The small bust, approximately 2 heads down, accents the narrow rib cage and small waist. Keep the shoulders slightly wider than the hips. The tummy is flat and the buttocks is small. The middle of the figure is at the crotch. From here, it is 2 heads to the knees. Draw the arms and legs long, and graceful. Never show distracting muscles on the fashion figure. The slim feet and narrow ankles are 2½ heads from the knees.

23

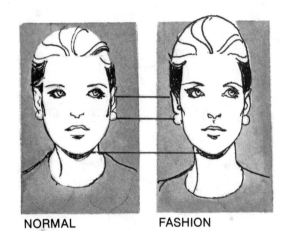

NORMAL   FASHION

Drawing the Female Fashion Head

The fashion head is the focal point of interest. It is a beautiful face that creates and sets the mood in communicating to the public the fashion story.

Working from photographs, keep the fashion head longer and slimmer than the normal head. Accent the cheekbones by drawing the temple slightly narrower. Keep the features soft, delicate and well shaped.

As a rule, when drawing the black fashion model, the only difference will be to show a wider nose and fuller lips. Careful attention should be given to the texture of the hair.

It has always been my feeling that there are no hard rules in drawing the fashion features. One artist may prefer to draw the eyes by indicating the iris with a circle. Another artist will use a black dot. What does it really matter, if it is a pretty eye?

24

EXAGGERATE THE
LONG ELLIPSE OF
THE EYELIDS

KEEP THE
CHIN SMALL

DO NOT INDICATE
TEETH IN THE
OPEN MOUTH

The Female Fashion Features

The fashion features can be rendered as a simple line drawing, or have a realistic approach that coordinates with the rest of the illustration.

The *eyes* are the most expressive feature of the fashion head. Study photographs of fashion models and notice the many moods that reach out to convey a message. The long ellipse of the eye can be exaggerated with long lashes, or with a thick black edge. Draw the eyebrow in a long pleasant arch.

The *nose* is usually drawn simply—with a subtle hint of the tip and nostril. A younger model will have a slightly upturned nose—whereas the sophisticated woman will have a straight nose.

The fashion *mouth* is drawn with the lower lip fuller than the upper lip. Keep the lip outline smooth and even. *Do not* indicate teeth in an open mouth.

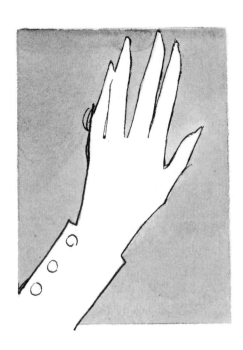

The Female Fashion Hand

For every fashion figure, the hands are a big part of the fashion story. They are used to create a fashion mood as well as being used to show the reader an important feature about the garment.

Keep the hands in relation to the elongated proportions of the fashion figure. The fingers are longer and slender. Avoid showing a lot of structural detail and bony knuckles. The top side of the hand is flat. A round hand will look fat and ungraceful.

Do not draw a foreshortened hand. Use a simple line to indicate long fingers. It is always helpful to look at tear sheets of other artists' work to see how they render a delicate fashion hand.

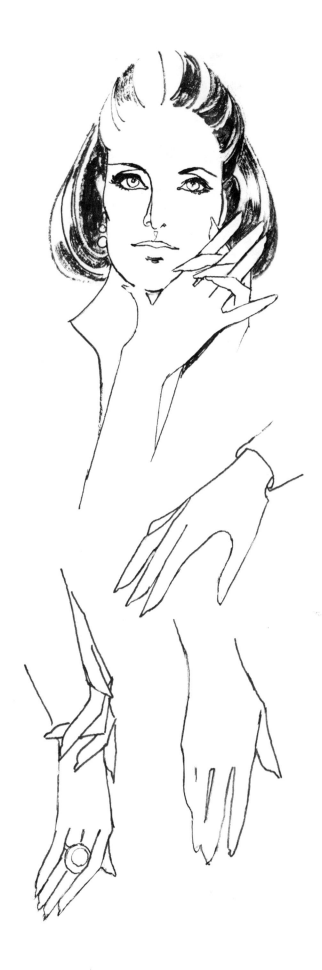

The Female Fashion Foot

Drawing the foot is very important to the total picture of the fashion illustration. The shoe must be stylish and must be suitable for the fashion apparel being featured. In spite of its importance, the shoe is not over-emphasized, but rather, it is an indication of being part of the foot.

Working from photos, learn to draw the foot with smooth contour lines. Avoid showing sharply pointed ankles, heels and toes. From the front view, show the outer bone as being prominent, extending in a smooth angle away from the ankle. Like the hands, the foot is long and slender and in its simplicity, is a beautiful part of a fashion drawing.

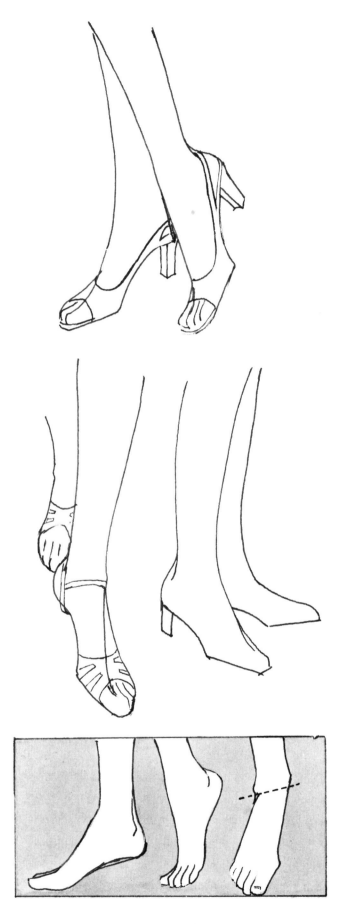

The Graceful Female Fashion Figure

For a smooth graceful flowing fashion figure select poses that are well balanced with the weight resting on one foot.

Study photographs of fashion models and look for poses that show shoulder and hip lines falling into opposite angles. Sometimes it is necessary to substitute the head from another photograph for a graceful figure.

Selecting Poses
for Each Garment

Besides drawing the fashion figure well, and learning to use the artist's materials, one of the most valuable skills comes in selecting the right pose for every garment the artist is called upon to sketch. *The pose must be selected to show off the most important detail of the garment.*

A *full and pleated skirt* should be illustrated in a pose that allows the skirt to swing freely for smooth, interesting lines.

A *narrow skirt* would be featured best in a pose that would have one side on a vertical line, as long as it did not take away from an important detail of the garment.

Clothes designed with the most important selling feature in the *back* should be posed from that position.

In *long fashions, robes* or *formal gowns,* the best pose will be the one that allows the fabric to hang in beautiful gravity folds.

The Fashion Folds

In keeping the fashion illustration simple, there are three basic folds that are used to show the garment to its best advantage.

The *construction* or *structure fold* remains constant, no matter what pose is used, for these folds are built into the design of the garment.

Gravity folds in fashion drawings are the most beautiful, for they fall freely from a point of suspension at one part or another on the body.

Action folds in fashion drawings should be drawn with the greatest care. Keep the folds simple, and use them to complement the design of the garment.

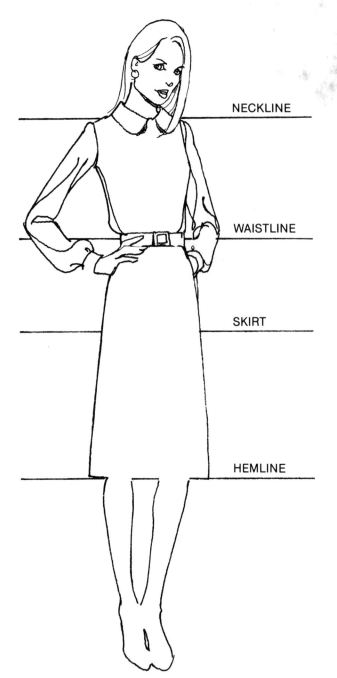

NECKLINE

WAISTLINE

SKIRT

HEMLINE

Important Areas of Women's Fashions

Every garment has at least one major detail that is the most important area to feature. The pose should be selected to show off that detail. Sometimes an important area to feature can be an oversized collar, a plunging neckline or large sleeves.

It is not often that the waistline will carry the whole fashion story, but care should be taken to show how it does relate to the main feature.

When drawing the skirt, exaggerate the full and pleated skirt to make it even more graceful. Pose the figure to show any side details, gathers and pockets.

The hemline is a very important detail in the fashion story. The hemline goes up and down every year. Keep up with the trends and know when these changes are taking place.

FOLLOW ARROWS FOR SWING OF SKIRT

The Skirt Swing Study fashion photographs to learn the many interesting ways to draw the fashion skirt. Remember one rule, the action of the hip and legs will determine how the skirt will fall. Keep the fold lines graceful and with different line directions.

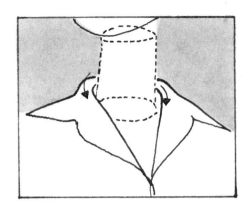

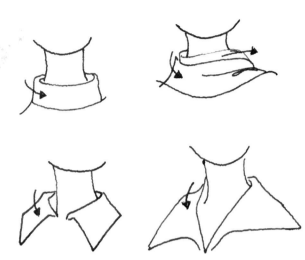

The Collar When fitting the garment on the neck, think of the neck as being a round cylinder, and curve the collar *around* it as the arrows indicate on the line art shown here.

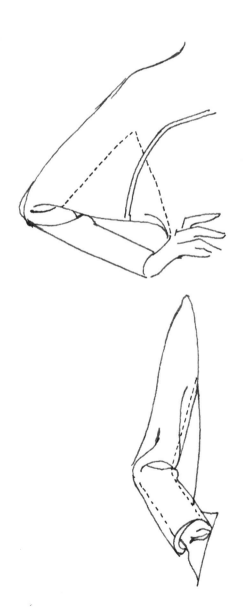

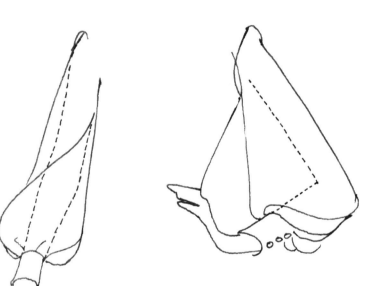

The Sleeve The sleeve is a very important part of the garment and should be drawn carefully. To draw sleeves successfully, it is a good rule to show, at one point or another, the fabric resting on the arm. This gives the sleeve support for a gravity fold or for a free falling construction fold. Exaggerate the full sleeve to create a more expensive look, and avoid showing a lot of folds. A lot of folds will make the sleeve appear wrinkled and ill-fitting.

35

Using Your
Reference File

When working from photos in your reference file the artist must learn to adjust the proportions, sometimes changing the position of the head and the swing of a skirt to get the graceful pose for a good fashion drawing.

The fundamentals of fashion art demonstrated in Unit 1 explain how working from photos can be of great value in learning to draw fashions.

This is not a new way of drawing fashion art. This is the way it is done in the professional world of

fashion illustrating. There are but a few artists who work directly from live models.

Working from photographs will still allow you to be creative, and to develop your own style and technique.

Most department stores supply their advertising department with display mannequins. This is very helpful in being able to put the garment on a model form to see how the garment fits and how the skirt will fall around the hips.

Drawing from Photographs

On the following pages you will see photographs and illustrations drawn from these photographs. In working from a photograph, notice how the proportions have been adjusted in the artwork. The neck is longer, the body is thinner, as well as the legs and feet.

The structure folds are evident in the illustration, since the folds are built into the design of the garment.

37

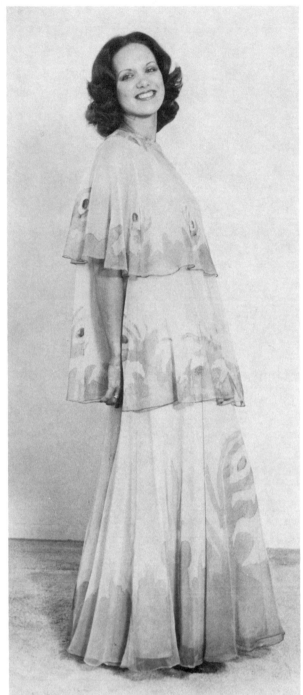

To add a touch of sophistication, the figure is drawn at 9½ heads tall. Note the simple lines of the hands and feet. The swing of the skirt has been exaggerated to emphasize the soft flowing fabric.

The gravity fold is evident here, as the weight of the fabric falls from the shoulders.

38

When drawing a dress ensemble such as the one shown here, show the structure folds of the dress. The head has been turned to achieve a more graceful pose.

The action folds are evident in the sleeves as the arms were moved back to show the pockets of the dress.

39

Leather An animal skin prepared for use by a tanning process. The important feature is that leather has a smooth slick surface. Sharp highlight areas are used to bring out the rich beauty of the leather.

Rendering Textures in Women's Fashions

Successful fashion artists have complete command of their approach in rendering fashion textures. Rendering textures is the final stage in which the fashion art comes alive and tells the customer what kind of fabric the garment is made of. The illustrations here were selected to show some of the many textures and techniques used in rendering fabrics.

Tweed A coarse-textured fabric in a variety of weaves and colors. A flat wash is applied first, followed by rough vertical and horizontal pen lines. Dark gray wash and white opaque flecks are used to show the character of this rough fabric.

Wool A soft fabric that is made of sheep's wool in both light- and heavyweights. Keep the base value light with a flat wash. The softness of the texture is shown with a darker wash in the shadow and fold areas. Keep the shadow areas and folds smooth and even.

Corduroy A pile fabric with lengthwise cords or wales. Using a flat tone as a base, draw the wales smooth and even with a thin wash line. The softness of this fabric can be seen in the shadow and fold areas.

Velvet and Satin Both velvet and satin are soft smooth fabrics that are rendered very much the same way with satin having the sharpest white highlight, and velvet having highlights blending together while the wash is wet. This same technique is used in rendering suede—using a dry brush effect to show the rich hues.

Knit A soft dull ribbed fabric in many thicknesses and weights. Used mostly for sweaters, the knit is indicated as shown in soft, even ribbing.

Glitter A flimsy, soft shining fabric made from metallic thread, or sequins sewn together. On large areas, do not show every round sequin— show dark and light wash areas with splashes of white and dark gray dots. Leave some areas of the garment white for shining highlights.

Chiffon A lightweight sheer fabric that falls into beautiful flowing folds. To show off the sheer fabric, the lightest wash areas are used on the outside edge. Therefore, the sleeves will show the arm through the fabric.

43

Helpful Hints in Rendering Fabric

The rendering of fabrics is as important as the drawing of the fashion figure itself. Many types of fabrics are available, and many new varieties are promoted each season. There are bold plaids and bright floral prints. There are soft fabrics and stiff fabrics, thick and thin fabrics. The renderings of all these various fabrics are governed by *one basic law.* Keep it *simple,* being careful to not overwork and show too many shades of gray wash.

Touch and feel fabrics. Study the direction of the weave and learn to simplify what is there. Practice and working experience will bring satisfying results.

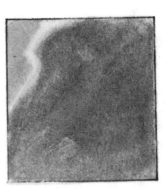

Velvet   Work in a fast easy motion, starting with a light gray wash. *Before* the first shade of wash dries a second shade of gray is added to the middle of the wet area. With black ink, carefully blend it into the still wet area.

It is important to have the highlight area worked out with a light pencil mark before beginning. After the wash is dry, carefully add fold lines and shadow areas.

Plaid   Look at the fabric. Learn to see it as a gray color. On a bright multi-color plaid, no more than three shades of color can be used. It is important that each wash is completely dry before another step is started. The first shade of gray, the lightest, is used on the background. Using a second shade of gray, the dominating stripe is applied. When it is dry, using the same gray wash, the stripe is painted horizontally. Add a black square where the stripes cross. Fine black pen lines are then added.

Using white opaque ink with brush or pen, the white stripes are added. Once the white opaque has been applied, the artist *cannot* add any more wet wash, as this would cause the white ink to run and smear.

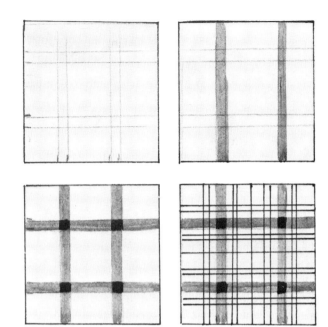

Floral   Using the same principle as for plaid fabrics, a flat gray is used for the background. (Many floral prints will have white background.) Use a second shade of gray for the floral outline. The third shade of gray is applied for the leaves and stems. *Be sure* that all shadow and fold areas are added before any white opaque ink is used.

Glitter   The highlight area is worked out on the art with a light pencil. A flat gray wash is used for the dark area, leaving the highlight area white (the board). Using a second shade of gray (or black pen line) the first set of lines are inked in the dark area. Using the same dark gray, small dots are added as shown. Using white opaque ink, the dots are painted to give the effect of glitter.

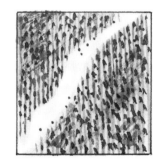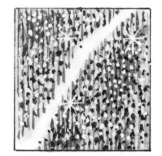

45

How to Render Fur Textures

There are many popular furs in fashion today. Furs are produced in many hair lengths and thicknesses of animal hair. It is very helpful to visit a fur salon. Let a fur dealer show you the inside of a fur coat. Notice the construction and how the pelts are sewn together. Look and compare the length of hair that some furs have. Your understanding of these details will help you render furs successfully.

To capture the beauty and richness of fur, the wet wash technique is popular with leading fashion illustrators. During all these steps the wash area *must* be wet.

 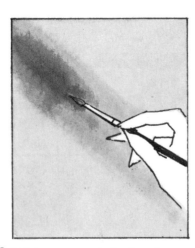 

1 Work one section at a time beginning with the collar. Wet the area thoroughly with a light gray tone.

2 With a second shade of gray wash, blend in several pelt areas.

3 A third shade of gray wash is added to the center pelt as shown. A dark wash line is applied to show the separation of pelts. When the artwork is completely dry, wipe most all the wash out of the brush and carefully add long strokes of fur along the edge.

46

Mink A short-haired fur, drawn here with a soft, wet on wet technique. The pelts are indicated with thin dark wash lines. The shadow areas are also blended by the wet wash technique.

Fox A long-haired fur, rendered here by soft shades of gray wash lines that follow the direction of the hair as it is draped over the shoulder.

Beaver A thick short-haired fur having a deep pile look similar to velvet. Rendered here with the outside edge lighter than the middle of the coat.

Chinchilla   A thick short-haired fur that is also rendered similar to velvet. After the wet technique has dried, a dry brush effect is used in the shadow and fold areas.

Persian Lamb   A thick tight curly-haired fur. In drawing this fur, a flat wash is used over the garment allowing it to dry before adding the curly texture with a dark wash. A dry brush effect is used in the shadow and fold areas to indicate the softness of the fur.

49

Rendering Lingerie

In rendering lingerie, the lines of the garment are kept fresh and delicate. There are several techniques used to achieve these effects, but for the best results use a combination of fine pen lines and wash.

Show all the special lace details on gowns and under clothes. Keep the line work on lace delicate, and avoid a lot of wash, for this will take away the freshness, as gray wash will make the garment look dirty. Select poses that show a slim and desirable figure. However, the figure should be drawn in such a way as to not offend any potential customers, or create an embarassingly revealing look.

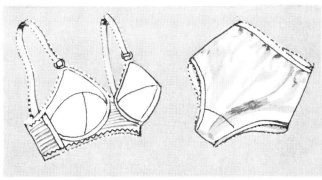

In drawing undergarments select poses that show the important construction features of the garment. The bodice of a slip, the cut of a bra, and the topstitching of a girdle are the distinctive details that a woman looks for in undergarments.

When drawing a brassiere *off* the figure, maintain the bustline as though it were on the figure. Show the topstitching as a broken line and all lace detail in a solid line. *Do not* use heavy ink lines, but rather, thin ink lines. On underpants, show the delicate lace details and the crotch structure.

51

Drawing Women's Fashion Sportswear

When selecting poses for sportswear merchandise designed for the active woman or the woman who likes casual clothes indoor or outdoor, show the figure in action or in a relaxed informal pose that the garment was intended for.

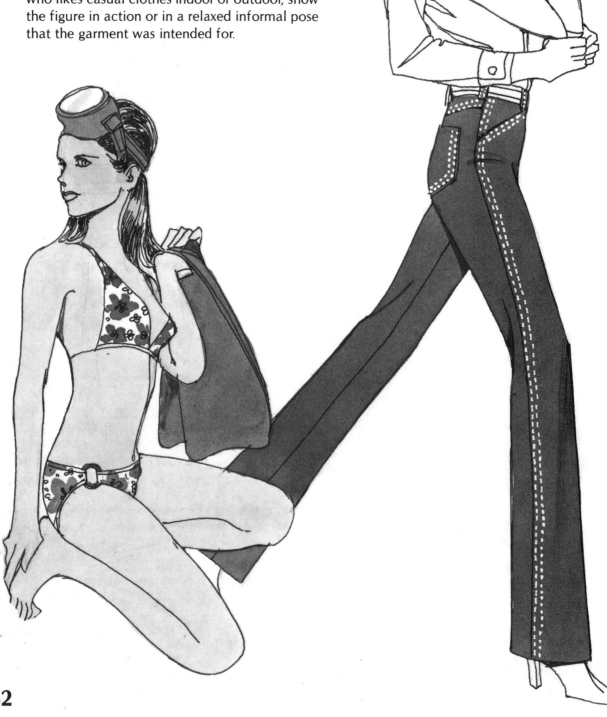

52

Add sports equipment to project the mood, carefully drawing the hair style as free and casual as the figure and activity suggests.

Drawing the
Junior Fashion Figure

The junior figure is drawn to show off their high-waisted bodies and long slender legs. Their stance, head action and facial expression can be exaggerated to show the independent person they have become. The proper hair style and accessories for this age group are best represented in *Seventeen* Magazine which can be more helpful than the more sophisticated high fashion magazines for your reference file.

Fashion Art Styles

There are two styles the fashion artist can use in rendering fashion illustrations.

1.   *Hard Sell* for the store that appeals to the price conscious customer.

2.   *High Fashion* look for the elegant store interested in appealing to the style conscious woman.

Hard Sell

In rendering hard-sell art, the garment is most always a popular-priced item in current demand, and one that will bring customers into the store to increase sales.

This fashion-illustration style is highly detailed. It shows off the construction of the garment and the print and texture of the fabric.

High Fashion

Simply elegant—for the elegant couturier specialty shop or department store carrying designer fashions. That is what high-fashion art represents. A mood is created to suggest a strong sense of individuality for the fashion-alert customer.

The style is loose, without a lot of detail on the garment. More emphasis is placed on the silhouette.

One photograph—many illustrative techniques. The illustrations on these two pages demonstrate just a few ways fashion artists create their own personal style.

Be alert to the unusual qualities that experienced fashion artists have that allow their work to have a distinctive style.

When working from photographs the artist is not trying for the same photographically detailed work. But rather, raising the quality of their work to an artistic expression. This is how technique can be developed from such an approach.

Study the fashion illustrations and display ads
found in magazines and newspapers to see how
artists establish a consistent image for the store
and a definite style for themselves.

Drawing Women's Fashion Accessories

Many fashion artists prefer to specialize in drawing fashion accessories. Because of their understanding of perspective, as well as skill in rendering texture, they are in great demand by department stores and accessory manufacturers.

Millinery   Before the artist can draw hats successfully it is important to know how to fit them on the head. Using the "see through" theory, as indicated here with dotted lines, the hat will fit the skull, and not the hair. Hats most always have one outstanding selling feature. And that is the angle to use when selecting the pose. Keep the faces pretty, and simply drawn to avoid distraction from the hat.

Handbags   Handbags are most always drawn in perspective to show two important features. The *front view* to show the opening and clasp, and the *side view* to show the depth and structure. Study illustrations and photographs, as well as the real merchandise, to see how the shoulder straps and handles are made. These are also the important features a woman looks for in selecting a purse.

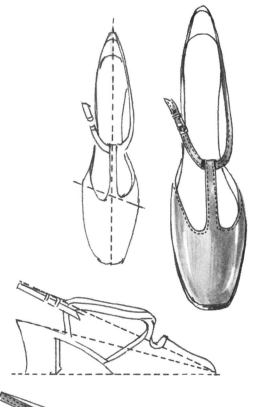

Shoes   Using the dotted diagrams as guides, the basic principles in drawing shoes can be understood. This is a highly specialized field, and a good shoe artist is hard to find.

Begin by working from illustrations. This is the way to get the feeling on how a shoe should be merchandised. It is important also to know how to draw the many kinds of leathers used to make shoes. The shoe is always drawn from the outside edge.

Jewelry Drawing jewelry requires more precision and accuracy than any other fashion art. *Do not* show every link, bead or stone. However, what is sketched should be drawn carefully and precisely. Jewelry is rendered best with a pen and ink, using small areas of light wash to show reflections and sparkles.

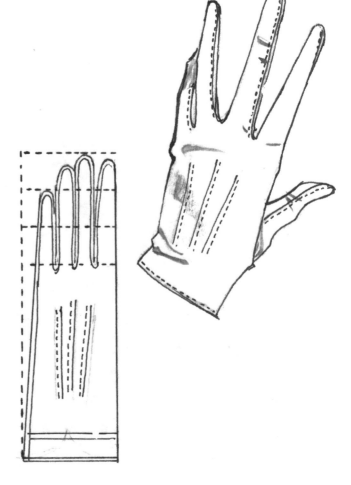

Gloves Illustrating gloves demands special care and attention to the structure and fingers to show off the detail of seamlines and topstitching. Keep the fingers long and slender on the female gloved hand. Avoid the use of too many shades of gray and heavy shadow areas. Study the flat diagram to understand the simple rules of drawing gloves off the hand.

Scarves Drawing a head and neck scarf can be more appealing and attractive by showing them being used around a pretty face. The illustration will show the customer how the scarf can be worn, and the gentle folds in the art add to the beauty of the merchandise.

Cosmetics Drawing bottles or cases for cosmetics require the knowledge of a few simple laws of perspective. The artist using the "see through" method can draw a good solid construction of the merchandise. With carefully drawn pen lines and controlled wash areas, the perfume bottle is turned into a beautiful piece of artwork that will create sales.

65

3 Illustrating Children's & Girls' Fashions

Specializing in Children's Fashions

If you like happy and active children then you might enjoy specializing in illustrating clothes for children. Drawing children's and girl's fashions is almost a branch of art in itself. On the following pages are important guidelines for drawing different age groups as they are classified in most department stores.

Remember that children's artwork is drawn to appeal to mothers who will be buying clothes for their children. Mothers reject artwork that shows children as being ugly.

Proportions for Different Age Groups

The proportions of small children are different in that their heads are quite large in relation to the length of their arms and legs.

At a year old, the arms and legs are quite short, even though their round body is about 3½ heads high. At eight years, the head has grown even larger and the child is at least 6½ heads tall. The tummy is still somewhat round. The legs are long and somewhat slimmer. It is at the age of twelve

and thirteen that children are about 7 heads high. The legs are again getting longer and slimmer. For girls the waist is now slim, and a small bust has developed.

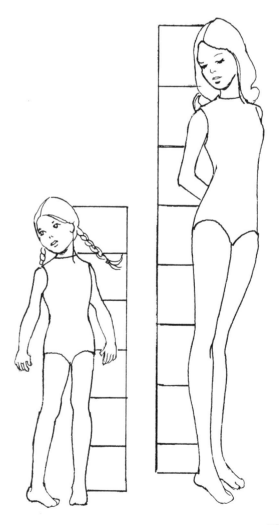

ROUND EYES

ROUND CHIN

ROUND CHEEK

ROUND FACE/
SHORT NECK

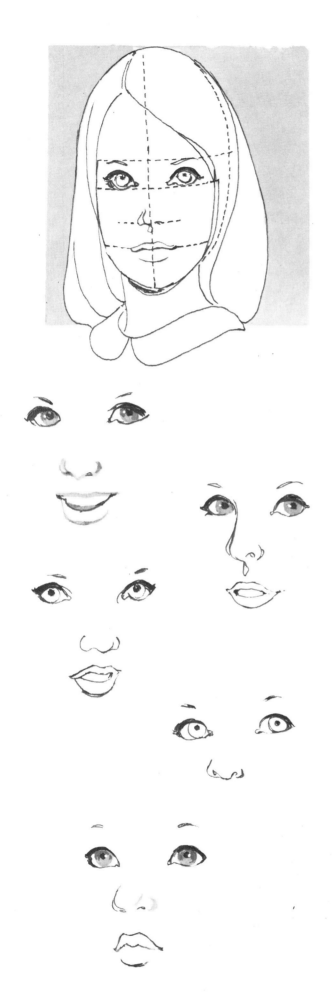

Drawing Girls' Fashion Features

Children are fast to express many feelings and emotions. And a lot of spirit lies in their faces. If you can capture these qualities on children's faces in your illustrations, you will be in great demand.

Study photographs of children. Notice the different age groups and how the facial structure changes from a baby to that of a teenager.

The *eyes* of children should be drawn with care. Keep them round, widely spaced. *Do not* show long lashes, but rather a dark line on the lids.

Eyebrows should be mere indicators, almost transparent, for a heavy line would make the children appear older.

The *nose* should also be treated with care, and drawn small and slightly upturned.

Full *lips* are always appealing for young girls, but on a baby it is best to show a small mouth that is pursed. *Do not* indicate teeth in an open mouth.

In young children, the *cheeks* are extended and round. This will remain until they reach their teenage years and the face begins to thin out and their chins become more pronounced.

INFANTS

TODDLERS

4-6X

7-14

Proportions & Poses for Children's Age Groups

Staff artists in department stores are required to sketch children's clothes in age groups that coordinate with manufacturers' size charts. And most children's wear buyers are willing to work with the artist to meet these requirements.

Infants   Most always infants are shown at the ages from eight months to twenty-four months. Even though some are able to stand and walk, they are illustrated in seated poses. The body is round and the arms and legs are chubby.

Toddlers   Between two and four years old the children are shown as still having a round body. The legs and arms are longer, but still plump. Keep the poses animated; that is typical in this age group.

4-6X   It is this group that girls like being dressed up. The body is getting taller, but still somewhat plump. Show the legs and arms as beginning to thin out.

7-14   This is the group that girls begin to be quite feminine and coy. Their bodies have begun to thin out and the legs are drawn long and slender. They are more particular about their hair styles and have developed good grooming habits.

Girls' Fashion
Hands & Feet

When drawing girls' hands and feet, keep the ink lines simple. Do not overdraw, or try to show a lot of detail. Each age group has its own hand action and foot stance that shows its spirit and character.

A small baby has short round fingers and thick chubby knuckles that are indicated with dimples. To emphasize a plump hand, show creases at the wrist. At the age of four, the hand has lost its baby appearance and the fingers are now thin and longer. By the time a child is seven years old the hand looks much like an adult's, only smaller.

The feet are carefully drawn in relation to the body. The two and four year olds have large, chubby feet. The foot begins to thin in the years between seven and fourteen. Show shoe styles that are popular. Keep the lines simple, in order not to take away from the garment being featured.

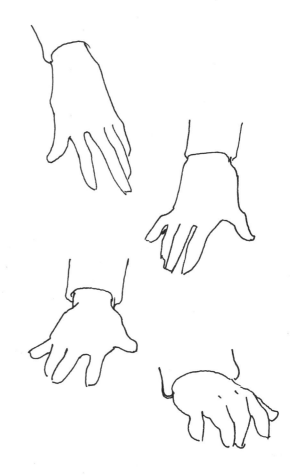

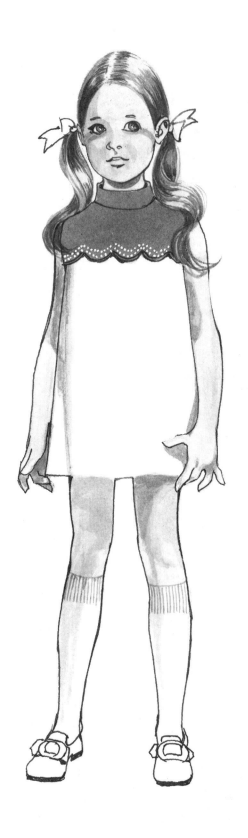

Drawing Girls' Fashions

Children's fashion artists are called upon to sketch many different garments. When showing dresses it is best to keep the poses feminine, and a hair style that is suitable for the occasion. Sometimes children are like little rebels, this can be appealing, and can put a smile on your face, as shown in the illustration below.

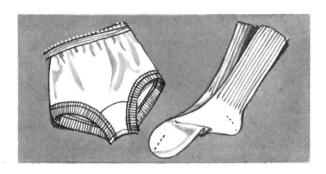

Panties and Stockings These are some of the garments advertised by department stores. There are several features that are shown when drawing panties. The leg openings and crotch seam are important, as well as lace details. Socks are most always the same, except for the length of the hose itself.

Infants' Wear When drawing infants' dresses, care should be given around the neck and sleeve areas. Exaggerate the fullness of the skirt to make it more attractive.

Drawing the Preteen Fashion Figure

There is an age group called preteen (sizes 12 to 14) that many department store buyers like to use for the girl in the seven to fourteen age group.

The figure at this age has started to mature. The head is almost full grown, a small bust has developed, and the waist has become smaller. The poses can be active or rather coy—for it is this age that a girl will develop her first crush. Because girls are very conscious of good grooming during this period, keep the hair style current.

Drawing the Teenage Fashion Figure

The teenage girl is flighty. She is also shy as well as sophisticated. Select poses that reflect these moods, for she does want to be different. Teen magazines will be a good source of information on poses as well as for current hair styles.

4 Illustrating Men's Fashions

Men's Fashions vs. Women's Fashions

The style of men's clothing does not change as rapidly as women's fashions. The suit itself is basically the same except for the changes in the width of the lapels; length, cut and opening of the jacket. The pockets are placed in the same area on the jacket but in different positions. The buttons are most always in the same place, except sometimes the trend will be for a two-buttoned suit or a three-buttoned suit. The double-breasted suit comes and goes as well as the vest.

The drawing of women's fashions can be exaggerated, even faked. But men's clothing, especially business suits, must be specific, more precise. It is important for the artist who wants to draw men's fashions to become familiar with the construction of men's clothing. The artwork will be more convincing if every fashion detail is carefully placed in its proper place.

Often an artist will not be able to draw men's and women's fashions equally well. For one reason, in a large advertising department there is enough men's fashion ads to keep one artist too busy to do anything else.

Another reason is that most artists like to draw pretty clothes, beautiful faces, bridal gowns, etc. They are not content with drawing "stale" fashions for men. So the desire to draw men's fashions is not there.

However, with the right attitude, and a good photo file of men's poses and action figures, drawing men's fashions can be just as exciting and fun.

In this unit, I will discuss drawing the male fashion figure, men's fashions and men's furnishings. In order to present a comprehensive text on fashion illustration, some information discussed in Unit 2, Drawing Women's Fashions, will be repeated in this unit on men's fashions. You will notice many similarities in drawing men's and women's fashion figures and fashions as well as many differences.

Proportions of the Male Fashion Figure

The male fashion proportions are lengthened much the same as the female. The height is 8½ heads high. The figure can be as much as 9 to 10½ heads high.

The male fashion figure has a narrow head. For a slim, masculine appearance, keep the shoulders broad and the hips narrow. The neck is not lengthened but remains the normal size.

NORMAL   FASHION

1
2
3
4
5
6
7
8
9
10

80

Posing
the Male
Fashion Figure

Select photographs of male models that are
masculine and well balanced. *Do not* use action
photos that will interfere with the lines of a suit.

As a guide to proper balance, start with a vertical
line beginning at the pit of the neck to the middle
of the foot supporting the body.

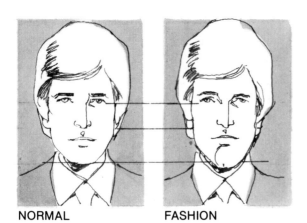

NORMAL   FASHION

Drawing the Male Fashion Head

The male fashion head has square and angular features. The illustration above shows the proportions of the fashion head in relation to the normal head.

The fashion head is slimmer and longer than the normal head. The chin is strong and square. Keep the ears small and close to the head. The neck on the fashion head is the same size as on the normal head.

The blocking in of the head is very important in locating the correct placement of the features. This will help you to draw heads in any position.

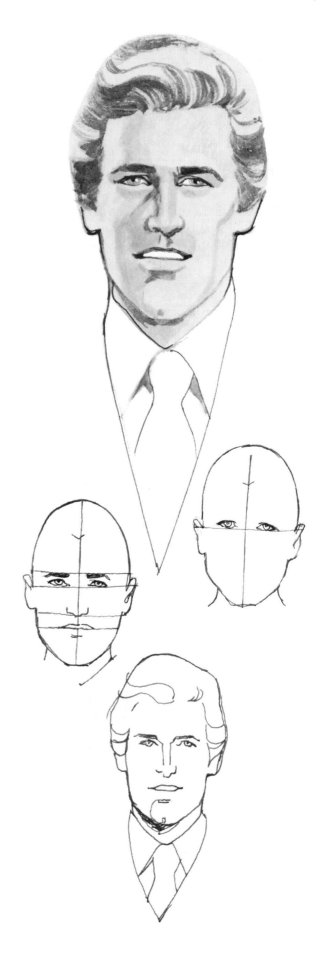

THE
NOSE IS
STRAIGHT

PROMINENT
BONES &
MUSCLES

THE UPPER
LIP IS THIN

DO NOT
INDICATE
TEETH IN
THE OPEN
MOUTH

The Male Fashion Features

The male fashion features can be rendered just as realistically as the female features. *Avoid* too much shading on a head that is going to be small when reproduced. A simple line drawing with or without a flat wash will be better.

When drawing the features, keep the *eyes* small, mere indications. When drawn open, keep the upper lid black. Do not show eyelashes. The eyebrows are heavy, straight and close to the eyes.

The *nose* is long with a simple indication of the angular nostril. The younger model has a fuller and upturned nose. The older man will have a more prominent nose.

Draw the *mouth* large with a well-shaped lower lip. The upper lip is drawn with a single thin line or outline. The mustache is rendered with a series of thin pen lines. *Do not* indicate teeth in an open mouth.

85

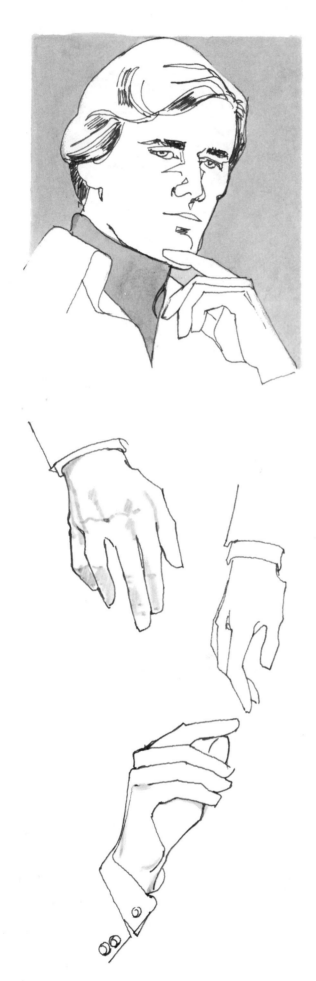

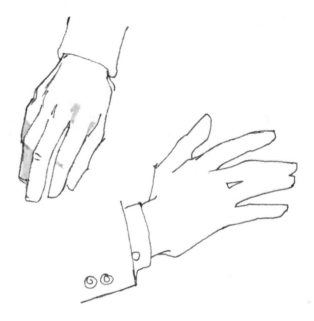

The Male
Fashion Hand

One of the most difficult parts of the anatomy to draw is the hands. Since fashion drawings show very little shading and construction, your fashion figures will appear weak if you do not understand hands and their anatomical construction. Keep a good anatomy book close by to use in your work.

The hands are used to express the feeling of masculinity as well as being used to bring out the selling features of the garment.

Do not elongate the hands as you would the female fashion hand. When working from photographs draw the male fashion hands normal size in relation to the rest of the body. The fingers are angular with the tips square. The knuckles and other bone structures are slightly suggested.

The Male Fashion Foot

The male foot and hands cannot be drawn in a simple form and as easily as the rest of the body. A good understanding of the muscles and bones will help the artist to draw the simple form which will represent the real foot.

Keep the foot slightly smaller and more slender than the photo will show. The shoe is simple, with a suggestion of the details. If the illustration has a wash on the garment and is carried to the cuff, the shoe should also have a wash with some shading.

The sole of the shoe is dark and flat, with a square toe line. Draw the inside edge with the arch high. Showing the inside of the heel is left to the preference of the artist.

Important Areas of Men's Fashions

When drawing women's clothing there is at least one major fashion detail that is featured. But in men's suits there are many styling details that must be carefully rendered.

The *shirt collar* fits the neck, and the length of the collar points should be in the current style.

The *tie* is selected to contrast with the fabric of the suit.

The *lapels* are drawn the correct width of the suit being featured.

The *closed suit jacket* is most always buttoned at the waistline.

The *length of the trousers* usually remains the same. It is the *width of the trouser* at the knees and cuffs that changes.

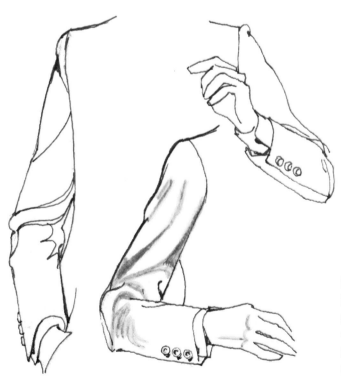

Sleeves Study men's fashion photos and notice how the folds and wrinkles add character to the garment. Simplify the art, avoid showing a lot of wrinkles; pick out a few major folds and let the rest of the sleeve be smooth. In men's clothing, the arm will move freely inside the sleeve. The arm in a bent position will touch the fabric.

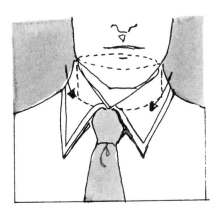

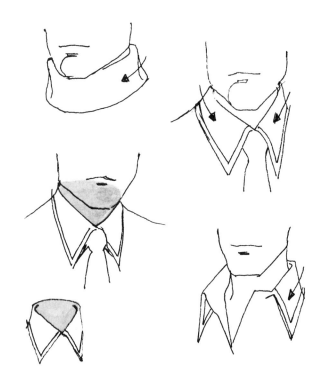

Collars The neck is a round cylinder. And the dress shirt collar, shaped like a triangle, fits around the neck with the back higher than the front. There is no space visible between the knot of the tie and the collar.

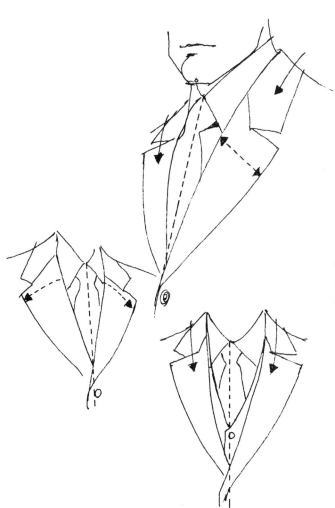

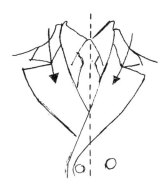

Lapels As a men's wear fashion artist you must examine the lines and details of the suit lapels and their fashion significance. The lapels are not straight hard lines on the suit. But rolled gently and curved, to fit the body under it. It is this style and fashion detail that sells the merchandise.

Suit Center Button This is in line with the neck point and the center of the tie.

Important Selling Features in Men's Suits

The most important selling features in drawing men's suits are explained on this page. Study them and learn how to apply them to your artwork.

The Jacket Line   When a pose is selected to show an important new jacket cut, keep the arm away from the figure. This is a construction feature, and the cut of the jacket (some years it is tapered up higher) is a big selling feature.

The Jacket Opening   Special care is given to the curve of the jacket opening. Some suit styles will be curved more, some cuts will be completely straight.

The Shoulderline   Keep the shoulderline wide and slightly slanted. The suit will appear to fit well at the neck when some of the shirt collar shows. Notice the hips are narrow in relation to the shoulders.

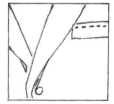

Jackets The correct position of the suit pocket is very important. It must be drawn as carefully as the depth of the flap itself is rendered.

Positioned over the heart is the breast pocket. It can be shown with or without a handkerchief tucked in.

Much of the suit design is concerned with the lapels. The most important changes in men's fashions take place in this area.

Count the buttons! It may seem like a small matter, but quite a significant part of the fashion story.

Use a fine ink line to indicate any topstitching detail. This is the "finishing" touch a suit needs for a smart fashion drawing.

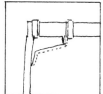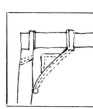

Belt Loops & Pockets Belt loops and pockets on men's trousers are also important areas of men's clothing. They should be drawn carefully, both in the preliminary pencil drawings as well as in the finished illustrations. The important consideration is being aware of the angle at which the pockets are placed.

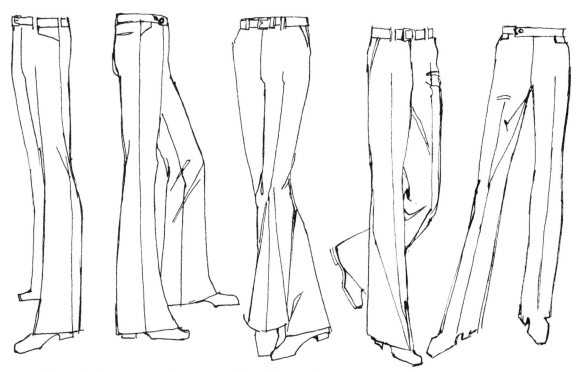

Trousers Many fashion artists have complained that drawing the trousers is one of the more difficult garments to illustrate. That is because you must draw the leg touching the trouser at one point or another, preferably at the knee.

If the leg is centered in the trouser, the pants leg will not hang or drape for interesting folds or crease lines. Be alert to the style changes in men's trousers. Some years the trousers are slim and tapered. Other years they will be gently flared.

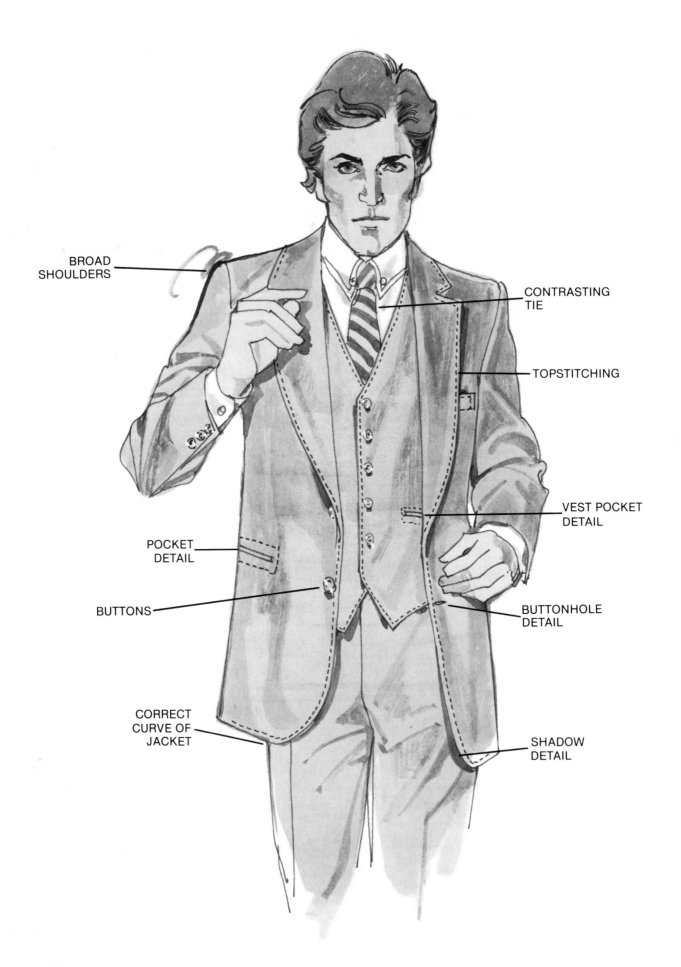

BROAD
SHOULDERS

CONTRASTING
TIE

TOPSTITCHING

POCKET
DETAIL

VEST POCKET
DETAIL

BUTTONS

BUTTONHOLE
DETAIL

CORRECT
CURVE OF
JACKET

SHADOW
DETAIL

92

Illustrated Summary of Important Men's Fashion Details

SUITABLE STYLE OF HAT

ROLLED COLLAR

SHOULDER TABS

BUTTONHOLE DETAILS

SHADOW UNDER BUTTON

BUCKLE

SLEEVE TAB

CONTRASTING NECKLINE

INTERESTING SHADOWS & FOLDS

CONTRASTING HANDKERCHIEF

LAPEL DETAIL

CUFF DETAIL

POCKET DETAIL

Drawing the Dress Shirt

Men's fashion artists are called on to draw dress and sport shirts more than any other single fashion garment.

The most important fashion feature on a shirt will be the collar. The length of the collar points and the curve of the collar demands special attention. It must be right!

As a staff artist, you will be expected to make these details accurate and if not, you can count on being asked to change the artwork until it is correct.

All dress shirts should be shown with a tie. At a glance a potential customer will know what kind of a shirt is being advertised. The sport shirt is drawn open at the neck.

The "floating" shirt is drawn in the same manner in which it is folded for displaying on the shelves.

Check all sleeve cuffs for button details. Like the collar, this is a significant fashion detail.

Dress shirts are rendered with a few soft fold lines. Keep the shirt clean, neat and crisp-looking.

Drawing Men's Active Sportswear

There has been a lot of excitement in men's casual clothing in the past few years. More leisure time, and the trend towards physical fitness have created a whole new field in men's wear.

Buy tennis, golf and other active sports' magazines to find new and exciting poses to illustrate active sportswear.

Be selective of your poses. The important thing is to show "neatly" the selling features of a garment.

96

Drawing Men's Furnishings

To show men's furnishings attractively you will need to look at the garments—their basic structure, shape and form. Be aware of how other artists "float" their merchandise.

Large garments such as robes are best featured on a figure. Small items such as undershirts, pants and hosiery are shown off the figure.

Keep the "floating" artwork flat and crisp. Use sharp ink lines and soft light shadows for folds and texture patterns.

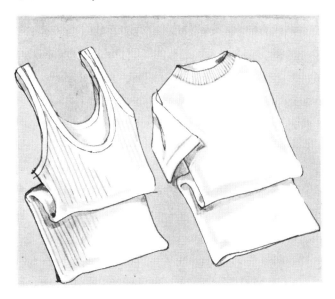

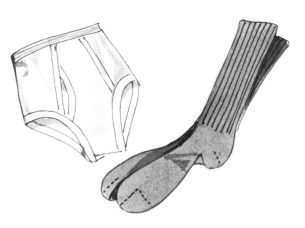

Rendering Textures in Men's Fashions

There has been over the past few years a greater selection of fabrics being used in men's apparel. It is important for the fashion illustrator to learn the details of line and tone to distinguish one fabric from another. As in women's fashions, rendering textures is the final stage in which fashion art comes alive and tells the customer what kind of fabric the garment is made of. The next few pages are just a few ways textures can be rendered. As you can see there are some fabrics used for men's and women's fashions.

Wool A soft fabric that is made of sheep's wool in both light- and heavyweights. The base value is kept light with a flat wash. The softness of the texture is shown with a darker wash in the shadow and fold areas.

Suede and Alpaca Kid or other leather finished with a soft napped surface having a rich-dull surface. Alpaca is a crisp animal fiber with a nubby pile texture. Used mostly as a trimming on sportswear or as a lining. In the illustration above suede is used for the jacket and alpaca for the collar.

Leather An animal skin prepared for use by a tanning process. The surface is slick, casting sharp highlights.

99

Tweed A coarse-textured fabric with vertical and horizontal stripes indicated with a dark wash on top of a flat wash. The use of white opaque flecks will bring out the character of this rough-textured fabric.

Sweater Knit A fabric made of interlacing loops of yarn produced in different weights and thicknesses. Show the ribbing with fine ink lines or gray wash; over these indicate the folds of the garment.

Rendering Weaves in Men's Fashions

Texture is the arrangement of the interwoven threads which make up a fabric—how it looks and how it feels to the touch. There are many weaves (the interlacing of threads and yarns that form a fabric) that have distinctive patterns.

This page illustrates a few of the more popular weaves in men's apparel, and the methods of rendering them. Also illustrated are some patterns and pile fabrics.

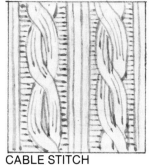

CABLE STITCH

CORDUROY

HERRINGBONE

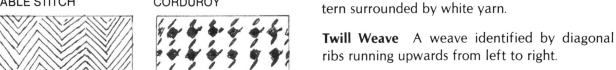

HOUNDSTOOTH

TWILL WEAVE

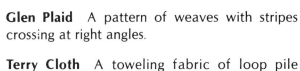

GLEN PLAID

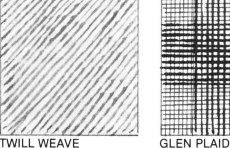

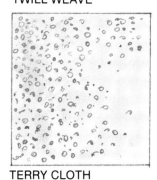

TERRY CLOTH

VELOUR

Cable Stitch   A knit pattern used on sweaters (and socks) resembling a twisted rope.

Corduroy   A fabric with narrow or wide cords or wales of raised yarns.

Herringbone   A broken weave resembling a "V" design.

Hound's Tooth Check   A four-pointed check pattern surrounded by white yarn.

Twill Weave   A weave identified by diagonal ribs running upwards from left to right.

Glen Plaid   A pattern of weaves with stripes crossing at right angles.

Terry Cloth   A toweling fabric of loop pile construction.

Velour   A soft woven fabric with a short velvety pile.

Drawing Men's Fashion Accessories

It is important for the artist to be alert for new styles and fashion trends in men's accessories.

Millinery Drawing men's hats in fashion illustrations or for an ad would depend on the timing. In some seasons, and maybe for several years, hats will be completely out of vogue. Then a new trend will pick up and hats will be seen again with suits, coats and sportswear.

The hat is drawn on the head correctly with the "see through" theory of dotted lines. The crown is drawn to fit the skull and not the hair. The hat, centered on the face, is shown with the brim drawn close to the eyebrow.

Gloves Gloves should be drawn carefully on tissue paper before transferring to illustration board. The line drawing here shows the principles that apply to all gloves, male and female. *Do not draw the fingers on the male glove as elongated as you would for women.* Show the stitching details along the seams as well as any fur or pile fabric lining.

Knit Hats and Mufflers Draw knit hats and mufflers around a handsome face. It suggests to the customer that the merchandise is a thick knit, warm, as well as attractive.

Leather Accessories Billfolds and other leather accessories, are drawn in perspective to show the carrying compartments for photographs and credit cards. These are the selling features a customer looks for when making a purchase.

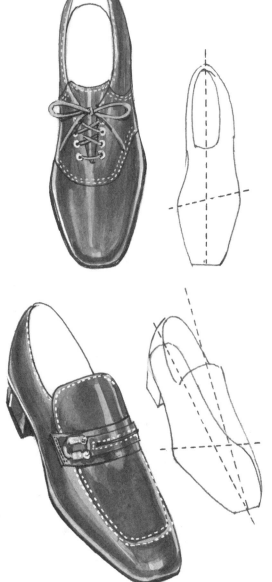

Shoes The most often used position for drawing shoes is the three-quarter view. The center guideline is determined with an outline indication of the sole. Draw the shoe carefully on tissue paper before transferring it onto the work area. Use several shades of gray wash to bring out the form of the shoe.

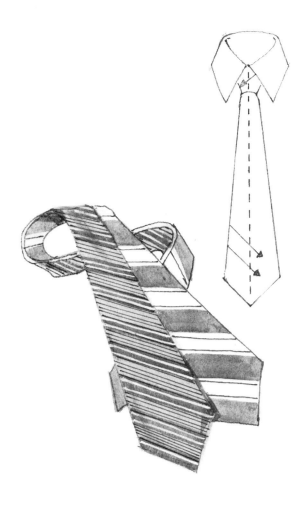

Ties The tie, when not shown on a figure, is placed in a "floating" position. Using a center guideline, the middle of the tie is determined, and in line with a right angle point. The width of the tie is a fashion feature and should be drawn correctly. Using the center guideline, work any pattern or stripe in uniform order.

Jewelry You learn to draw jewelry by quietly observing the merchandise. Pick it up, look it over. Jewelry should be drawn carefully with as much accuracy as possible. Moving the jewelry around you will catch the reflections to highlight on your artwork.

Belts Belts are most always drawn flat with a slight wave in the strap. Draw the buckle with an edge to show dimension. Use a flat wash and black areas to show highlights in the buckle and the texture of the belt.

Drawing University Shop Fashion Merchandise

The University Shop merchandise is geared for the young college-bound male. The clothes are fashionable and somewhat youthful. The cut of this merchandise is for the smaller, slender figure. It is this cut also that attracts the older customer who needs a smaller fit.

The proportions for the University Shop male fashion figure is 8½ heads high. The shoulders are not as broad, and the head and neck will remain normal size.

The face is youthful with a short upturned nose and fuller lips.

The clothes are casual, properly accessorized for this age group. Be sure that the shoes are the current style and appropriate to the merchandise being advertised.

5 Illustrating Boys' Fashions

The Appeal in Boys' Fashion Illustrations

Much of the appeal in boys' fashion illustrations comes from how the artist feels about the subjects themselves.

Besides understanding the proportions of young boys, the artist must be able to project the appealing personality and character of young boys.

Boys are truly themselves, active, happy—and yes, full of mischief. A small boy is also beautiful in repose. These are the characteristics in artwork that will stop the eyes of mothers shopping for clothes for their children.

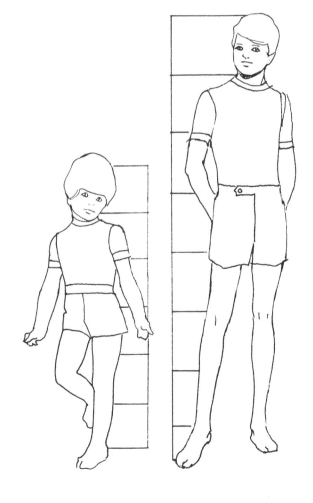

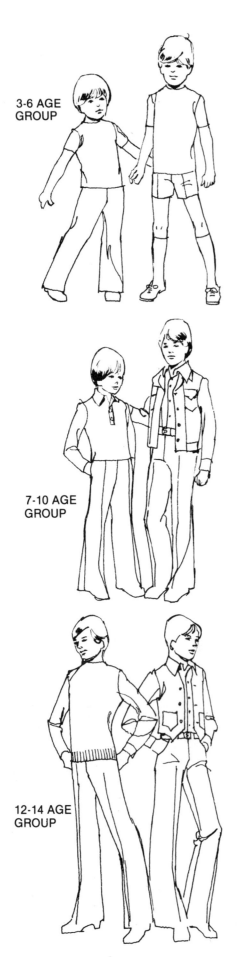

Proportions & Poses for Boys' Age Groups

Demonstrated on this page are the important proportions and poses typical of boys at different ages. These guidelines will help the artist to become familiar with manufacturers' size charts when drawing boys' clothing.

The proportions of small boys are very much like girls in that their heads are also quite large in relation to the length of their arms and legs. It is about the age of nine and ten that the character of the head is established and looks like an adult. By the age of thirteen and fourteen the head is full grown, even though the body is not.

3-6 Age Group   In this age group the boys have a large head and a round body. The arms and legs are slightly plump.

7-10 Age Group   The age of freckles and unruly hair. The character of the head is established and the boys' head looks like an adult. Draw the eyes large and the corner of the jaw round to keep the face young-looking. The body is beginning to thin now with long arms and legs. The feet are large in relation to the rest of the body.

12-14 Age Group   This is the age group when the boys are now "manly." They are conscious of their hair styles and wear shirts tucked in. The boy is tall and quite slender.

Boys' Fashion
Hands & Feet

Keep it simple! Young boys' hands and feet *should not* be drawn with a heavy outline, large knuckles, and lots of shading. These techniques age the hands and certainly would draw attention away from the merchandise. Buy family magazines and study the hands and feet (as well as the faces) of young children. Clip the photos and file them for reference work. Notice the action of hands and feet in the different age groups.

The feet should be drawn with just as much care as the hands. Be alert to what is smart in shoes and what styles to draw for every outfit. The right selection will add charm and character to your illustrations.

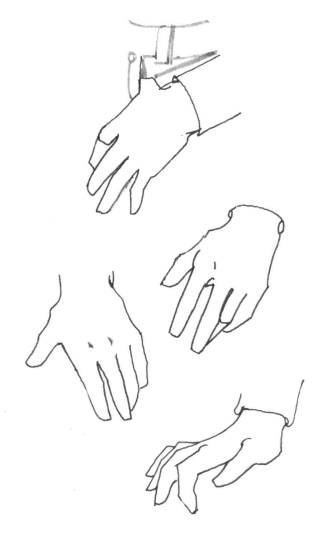

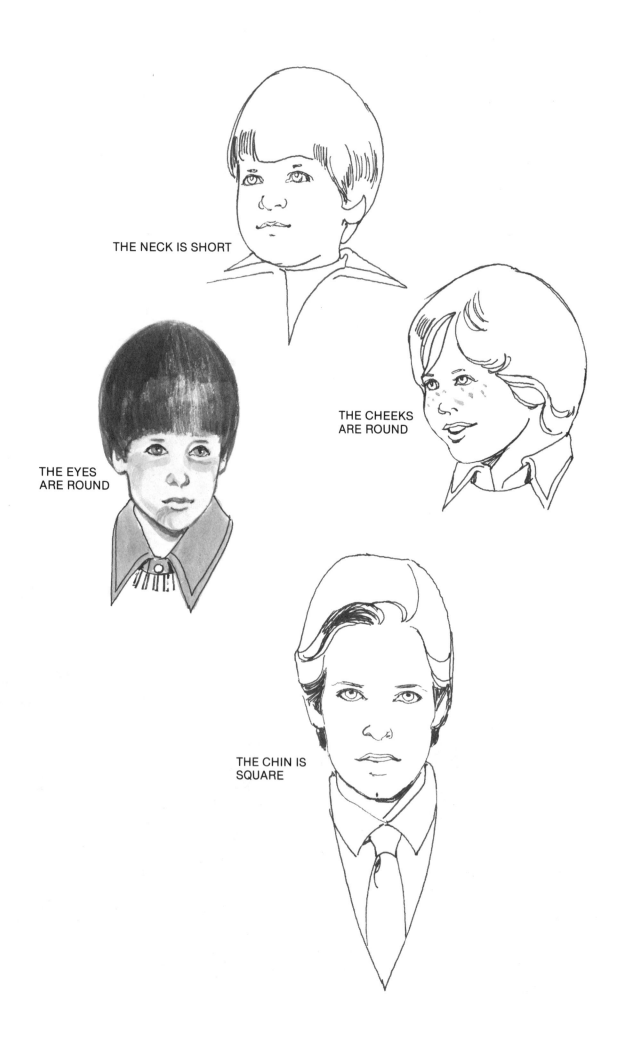

THE NECK IS SHORT

THE CHEEKS
ARE ROUND

THE EYES
ARE ROUND

THE CHIN IS
SQUARE

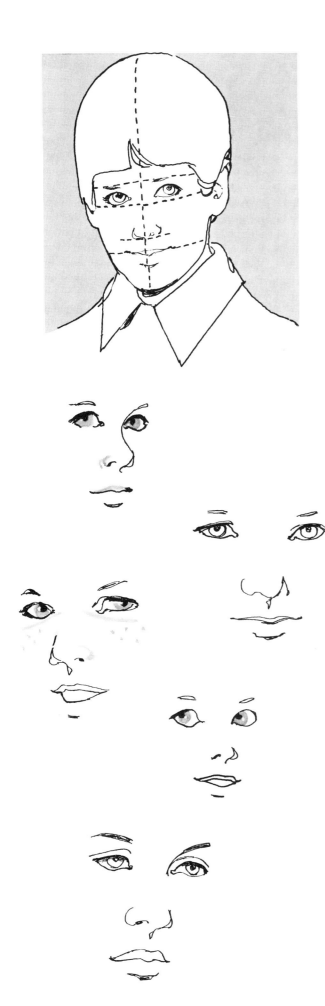

Drawing Boys' Fashion Features

A child's expression is much easier to capture when working from photos. The mischief in their eyes, and the charm of their smile is lightning fast.

Learn the many distinctive characteristics and personalities of children. They have many feelings and emotions and do not hide them as easily as adults.

Draw the boys' head large in relation to the rest of their body. The *cheeks* do not have definition for they are round and smooth.

The *eyes* are shaped much like buttons, alert and full of excitement. Keep the *eyebrows* thin and slightly arched. The *nose* is short and upturned. Do not make the *lips* too large for the face, as this will age him and make him look like an adult.

113

Illustrating Boys Realistically

There is always a certain appeal in artwork with a realistic technique. The more realistic artwork demands the merchandise be drawn just as accurately.

The right choice of hair style and sports equipment will add character to your artwork when drawing active sportswear. However, do not draw a football in a boy's hand during baseball season.

Using a free, loose technique on the face below shows a good contrast between the model and merchandise that is quite bold.

The books under the arm suggests the garment is for going back to school.

These poses represent typical young boys' fashion illustrations. Note the proportions of the head to the rest of the body. *Note* how the shape of the eyes and the round jawline keeps the face youthful looking.

Drawing the Young Male Fashion Figure

The male of sixteen to eighteen is now a young man. The fashion figure is about 7½ heads tall. The shoulders and arms are muscular, but not fully developed as in a full-grown man.

The poses are masculine and the styling of the merchandise is the same as men's clothing.

The proportions of the head to the rest of the body is still somewhat large. The face is no longer round, but angular. The eyebrows are thicker and the lips well shaped. The nose is drawn upturned to keep the face youthful.

Draw the chin square. The corner of the jaw is round and will not be fully developed until the age of twenty or twenty-one.

Jeans and vests have been a most popular outfit for high school boys for many years now. Select casual poses that will bring out the straight lines of the vest and the gentle flare of the jeans. Notice the styling detail in the topstitching and the shadow treatment of the jeans on their flared silhouette.

Select active poses for sportswear merchandise using sports equipment that the garment was designed for.

6 Reproducing Fashion Art

Reproduction

A fashion artist's work is reproduced in daily newspapers and magazines. An understanding of how artwork is prepared for newspaper printing will be helpful in achieving the best results for your art.

Many department stores are equipped to produce their own camera-ready artwork with a screened velox machine which makes line and halftone copies of artwork for newspaper printing.

There are two kinds of veloxes:

1. Line

2. Halftone

Line Velox A *line velox* is used to reproduce artwork having only ink lines and areas of solid black. This is the simplest form of reproduction and it is especially good for newspapers.

Halftone Velox The *halftone velox* allows the artist to use only gray wash on the artwork. The velox machine reproduces the artwork into dots by a 65-line screen in the camera between the lens and the photographic paper. The parallel lines of the screen (much like that of a window screen) photographs the tonal image of the illustration into areas that are merely dots.

The velox is developed and the dots, in keeping with the tonal values of the original art, are so close together that the untrained eye will see the picture as a whole, rather than a succession of individual dots.

Line Reproduction

Shown here is a line drawing from which a line velox was made. Using pen and ink, a halftone effect of tweed was created by the use of fine uneven lines. An enlarged area of the artwork is shown to illustrate the lines and areas of solid black.

Halftone Reproduction

A square halftone velox of the tonal drawing in wash is shown here. This is the same process used in reproducing a photograph. You will note in the enlarged area the variation of dots blending together for its tonal value.

For excellent reproduction, an engraving solution is used with water in the wash. The white areas will drop out and prevent the artwork from looking dull.

Line & Halftone Reproduction

When the artwork is rendered in both ink line and wash as shown here, it must be reproduced as a combination line and halftone velox. The art is photographed the same as a square halftone, with an extra shot taken for the black line and combined on one velox. The *tone areas* on the garment *are made up of dots,* and the *black lines* on the face and hairdo are solid black—having *no screen dots.*

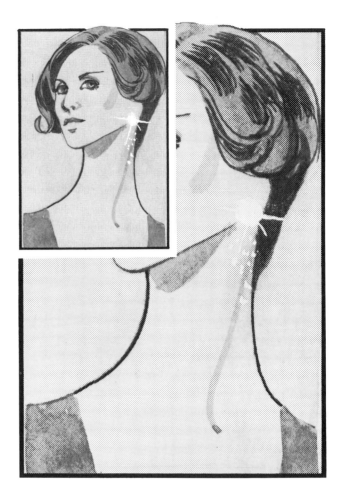

Tonal Chart

The chart here is a guide for the artist using gray wash when preparing artwork for newspapers.

Using three shades of gray, solid black and white areas will give the artist pleasing results when used properly. Keep the contrast between the grays sharp and clear on the artwork, and the chances are your art will reproduce well everytime.

7 Seeking A Job

A Closing Chat

There is something very rewarding and very satisfying for the fashion artist working in a department store. For one thing, you are part of a team of creative people all working together to produce effective store advertising. The better the store, the better the talent—the real pros in the business.

It is a challenge to take a garment and illustrate it the way you know that it will attract and persuade people to come to your store to buy it.

And the response is immediate, many times the very day the ad appears in the newspaper, and certainly for several days after.

The department store's art department is not a place for creative people to play prima donna. The copy writer, art director, layout artist and the fashion artist all work together, for every ad has one important objective—to sell—for the store that they work for.

Preparing Your Resume & Portfolio

There are two things which are essential to the artist pursuing a job as a fashion artist:

1. A good resume
2. An impressive portfolio

Resume It is always a good idea to use a professional resume service for preparing your resume. And for several reasons. They will keep to relevant details—your education, any previous full-time or free-lance employment, your job objective and a short paragraph on what you feel you have to contribute to a future employer. This professional service knows that the employer is interested in what you can do for them, as well as what you have done. A resume service will prevent you—tactfully—from listing any talent that you think you have, but do not. Not only do they "say it better," they also do a professional job of typing and reproducing copies.

Portfolio The portfolio should confine itself to ten or twelve of your best fashion drawings. Select samples that show you know how to handle wash and line drawings, as well as how you draw the fashion figure. Always call for an appointment to show your portfolio. See the advertising manager or art director. The personnel department is not qualified to judge your portfolio. *Do not* take up their time with endless chatter and artwork that is cluttered with several protective flaps that have to be lifted and replaced each time. The art director is much too busy!

For an impressive portfolio, purchase a binder that has clear acetate sheets in which to slide your artwork between. Not a photo album, but a presentation binder. You can find this in almost any art supply store. Resist *all* temptation to show other samples of artwork that do not relate to fashion art. A beautiful oil painting of a countryside does not reflect your fashion ability. Your future employer wants to know how you will render his merchandise in newspaper ads. Show him!

124

Glossary of Fabric & Advertising Terms

A

ACETATE   A man-made fiber used in linings.

ACRYLIC   A man-made fiber with a soft, woolly hand. Used in knit shirts, sweaters and slacks for warmth.

ADVERTISING   Any paid, nonpersonal message by an identified sponsor; appears in media and used to influence sales, services, or the acceptance of ideas by potential buyers.

ADVERTISING AGENCY   An organization which renders advertising (and marketing) services to clients.

ADVERTISING CAMPAIGN   Series of advertising messages devoted to a single theme, concept or idea with a definite objective.

ADVERTISING DIRECTOR   The person in charge of personnel and activities of the advertising department. Sometimes display and publicity are included in his responsibilities.

ALL WOOL   A term used to indicate a garment is constructed of wool only.

APPEAL   Motive to which advertising is directed, designed to stimulate action by the audience. Points made in copy to meet customer's needs and objectives, and provide reasons to buy.

APPROACH   Manner of presentation of appeals as determined by copywriter. Can be factual, imaginative or combination of the two.

ARGYLE   A diamond-shaped knitted pattern with three or more colors. Used for socks and sweaters.

ART   An element of print advertising. Includes wash illustrations or line drawings and photography.

AUDIENCE   People reached by an advertising medium.

AUDIENCE COMPOSITION, AUDIENCE PROFILE   The number of people reached by advertising according to age, sex, income, home, etc.

B

BALANCE (FORMAL)   Used in advertising layout when a dominant point of interest is desired with subordinate elements to develop equal attention power.

BALANCE (INFORMAL)   Attention is gained by dynamic balance in arrangement of elements. The difference in attention power is caused by shape, color or arrangement, often with dissimilar units.

BATISTE   A shirting and blouse fabric, sheer, of quality yarns, in a plain weave.

BLACK AND WHITE   Printing on white paper with black ink (or vice versa). No color is used. Also known as monotone.

BLENDS   The combination of different fibers to achieve improved color and performance.

BODY COPY   The main paragraph(s) of copy in an advertisement.

BOLD-FACED TYPE   Style of darker, heavier type; bolder and thicker than regular type.

BROADCLOTH   A tightly woven fabric in cotton or cotton blend. Used in shirts.

BROCHURE   Elaborate advertising folder or booklet.

C

CAMEL HAIR   Wool-like hair of the camel, expensive and soft to the touch. Used for coats, suits and sweaters.

CAPTION   Headline of an advertisement, or descriptive matter accompanying an illustration.

125

CASHMERE A fine soft wool obtained from the Kashmir goat. Used for sweaters, suits and coats.

CENTER SPREAD Two facing pages in center-fold of a newspaper or magazine.

COLD TYPE Type set by typewriter or by electronic or photographic process, not using molten metal. Used in lithographic (offset) printing and often in letterpress.

COOPERATIVE ADVERTISING Advertising run by a local advertiser in conjunction with a national advertiser. Cost is shared. The names of participants appear in the advertisement.

COPY All the words in an advertisement. Some define this as any material used in an ad.

COTTON A fabric produced from the seed pod of a cotton plant. This is one of the oldest apparel materials.

CROP Trimming of illustration to eliminate non-essential background or detail to fit desired allocated space.

D

DENIM A cotton or blended fabric identified by its diagonal rib running upward from left to right.

DOUBLE KNIT The fabric, used for pants, skirts and suits, is made on a circular knitting machine. It is stretchable and wash-and-wear.

E

EDITING Review, correction, and (ideally) improvement in copy.

F

FASHION OFFICE Department in larger retail stores where fashion planning and fashion coordination between departments is centralized.

FELT A fabric made from a combination of mechanical and chemical joining of fibers. Not woven.

FOLDER Printed circular, folded and often used as a mailing piece.

FORMAT In print, the shape, style, size and appearance of a publication.

FOUR-COLOR PROCESS Photoengraving procedure for reproducing color illustrations. This is done by a set of plates known as process plates; each prints one color: yellow, blue (cyan), red (magenta), black. Sequence varies, but together they produce full color printing.

G

GABARDINE A tightly woven fabric with twill pattern and diagonal rib.

GLOSSY Photograph with a shiny surface or finish, necessary for reproduction in print.

GRAPHICS Illustrations, art, diagrams, charts.

GRAVURE Any of the processes of printing from a metal intaglio plate, as distinct from letterpress print.

GUTTER Normally, the vertical unprinted area between facing pages and beyond copy and illustration.

H

HALFTONE Photoengraving plate photographed through a glass screen in the camera. Breaks up the reproduction of the subject into dots (or screen), making possible the printing of shaded values, such as in a photograph or wash illustration.

HEADLINE Major copy caption above text. The most important copy element in print advertising; usually, largest display type in ad.

HOT TYPE Metal printing type which when cooled is used for letterpress printing.

HOUSE BRAND Merchandise that bears a retailer's own name brand rather than that of a manufacturer's.

I

IMAGE Real or imaginary impression of the public of a product brand, or the reputation of an organization.

INTAGLIO PRINTING Printing from depressed surfaces as on a copper or steel plate. Rotogravure is a form of intaglio printing used for some newspaper magazine supplements.

L

LAMB'S WOOL   A soft wool sheared from a young sheep. Also known as fleece.

LAYOUT   A working drawing showing how an advertisement will look with all the elements in position; a guide to those who work on copy, art and production.

LETTERPRESS   Printing from a raised (or relief) surface. Ink comes in contact with raised elements and in direct contact with paper, similar to a rubber stamp.

LINE DRAWING   Illustration made with pen, pencil, brush or crayon for print advertising, composed of lines or crosshatch lines in imitation of shading. Variation in tone is indicated only by the width of the lines.

LITHOGRAPHY (OFFSET)   Printing from a level or flat surface on which non-printing areas are chemically treated to repel ink and to attract water. Ink and water are spread on plate from respective "fountains" while press runs. Thin and flexible plates are used to "offset" the image to a rubber blanket, which then transfers the image to paper.

LINEN   An absorbent, lustrous fabric that wrinkles easily.

M

MARKET   Any group with the desire and ability to buy.

MECHANICAL   All elements of an advertisement, proofs of type and illustrations, photos, etc. pasted in final arrangement (usually on illustration board), ready for camera. Photography is then used to make printing plate.

MERCHANDISE MANAGER   The executive who supervises a group of store buyers (not consumers).

MOHAIR   A lustrous wool from the Angora goat. It is stronger than wool. Used mostly for sweaters.

MOTIVE   Some inner drive, impulse, intention that causes a person to do something or to act in a certain way.

MERCHANDISING   The buying and selling functions of a retailer designed to present the right product, at the right time, at the right price.

N

NYLON   A washable man-made fiber that has strength and elasticity.

O

OFFSET   See *lithography*.

OXFORD   A soft shirting fabric having a basket weave.

P

PASTE-UP   See *mechanical*.

PHOTOENGRAVING   The metal form from which an advertisement can be printed. Also known as engraving, cut or plate.

POLYESTER   Man-made fiber of petroleum products. It is quick drying, crease resistant, and needs only minimum care.

PROOF   Copy of an advertisement *before* it is printed. Many proofs are made so that every person and department involved in the advertisement has the opportunity to check for accuracy before ad is actually run. Corrections are made before ad appears in print in a publication.

PUBLICITY   Unsponsored by source, non-paid messages, verbal or written in public information media about a company, its policies, personnel, activities or services.

R

RAYON   A man-made fiber of regenerated cellulose from trees. Feels like silk.

REPRINT   Reproduction(s) of an advertisement.

R.O.P., RUN OF PAPER   Advertising that appears in any place, on any page of a newspaper as determined by the paper's managing editor.

ROUGH   In the production of layouts, the first crude sketch to show the basic idea or arrangement of an advertisement.

S

SCREEN A fine cross-ruled sheet used in photo-mechanical platemaking process to produce tone in advertisements such as shades of gray. The size and number of dots on a screen reproduce different gradations of shading. More dots or fewer to the square inch give different values of gray shadings. See *halftone*.

SEERSUCKER A permanent woven crinkled or puckered cotton, usually in vertical stripes.

SHETLAND Soft tweeds made from the wool of the Shetland sheep.

SILK A natural continuous filament fiber produced by silkworms.

SINGLE KNIT A fabric used mostly for T-shirts and other sport shirts. Knitted on a single needle machine.

SPANDEX Used in active sportswear, this is a man-made elastic fiber with built-in stretch.

SPREAD Double-page advertisement on two facing pages. When this occurs in the center pages of a publication, the print may extend into the "gutter." This is called a center spread. This involves a higher cost for both plates and space. See *gutter*.

T

TABLOID Newspaper about half the size of a standard-size paper.

TAFFETA A lustrous fabric with a plain weave, smooth on both sides.

TEAR SHEET Copy of an advertisement after publication, torn from the actual publication. Positive proof of publication.

THERMAL An insulating fabric with a waffle-knit look. Used in underwear and pajamas.

TRICOT A knit fabric that is run-proof and is stretchable.

TYPEFACE The design and style of letters in type of a "family." Usually named for the designer.

TYPO The trade term for an error in type.

W

WASH ILLUSTRATION Brush work that produces a softer picture, made with a brush and diluted India ink or watercolor. Offers varying gray tones. Halftones must be used to reproduce.

WHITE SPACE Areas in an advertisement where no printing or illustration appear. Uninked areas.

Index

129